CLOISTERS

CLOISTERS

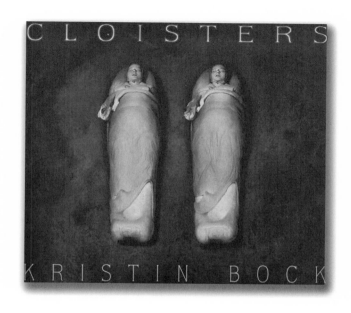

KRISTIN BOCK

TUPELO PRESS

Cloisters
Copyright © 2008 Kristin Bock
ISBN: 978-1-932195-55-2
Printed in Canada.   All rights reserved.
No part of this book may be reproduced without
the permission of the publisher.

First paperback edition, October 2008
Library of Congress Control Number: 2008926703
Tupelo Press, Inc.
PO Box 539, Dorset, Vermont 05251
tupelopress.org

Cover and text designed by William Kuch, WK Graphic Design

Cover painting: "Sleeping Twins" © Odd Nerdrum, courtesy of Forum Gallery,
New York and Los Angeles

Tupelo Press is an award-winning independent literary press that publishes fine
fiction, non-fiction and poetry in books that are as much a joy to hold
as they are to read.

Tupelo Press is a registered 501(c)3 non-profit organization and relies
on donations to carry out its mission of publishing extraordinary work that may be
outside the realm of the large commercial publisher.

for my parents,
Lorraine and Robert Bock,

& for Geoffrey

Acknowledgments

Grateful acknowledgment is made to the editors of the following
publications where poems or versions of these poems first appeared:

The Black Warrior Review: "Oracle"
Columbia: "Portrait of the Artist with Rossetti's Sitter," "Pastoral"
The Cream City Review: "Scarecrow"
Fence: "Amor Vincit Omnia"
Gulf Coast: "Notes from the Boat Docks"
The Hayden's Ferry Review: "Return"
Margie: The American Journal of Poetry: "Under the Ghost Tree," "Nostrum"
The Massachusetts Review: "Windscape"
Pleiades: "Before Poetry"
Prairie Schooner: "Restoring the Fourteen Stations of the Cross," "Phrenology"
Quarterly West: "Wintering"
The Seattle Review: "Each Light and Shade a Solitude"
Third Coast: "The Somniloquy of the Sleeping Asp," "Green Running through
  the Figure"

My sincerest gratitude to the Massachusetts Cultural Council for their support and
Tupelo Press for their continued support and encouragement.

I would like to extend great thanks to Agha Shahid Ali, Lisa Beskin, Corwin Ericson,
Lorna Hanes, Elizabeth Hughey, Caroline Lewis, Lori Shine, David St. John, James
Tate, Dara Wier, and my beloved P-Gals and Po-Group for their keen eyes and hearts.

Contents

One

Two

Three

Four

Five

August

ONE

October

like bees drowsing
         on doorknobs
we dropped away

On Reflection

Far from the din of the articulated world,
I wanted to be content in an empty room—
a barn on the hillside like a bone,
a limbo of afternoons strung together like cardboard boxes,
to be free of your image—
crown of bees, pail of black water
staggering through the pitiful corn.
I can't always see through it.
The mind is a pond layered in lilies.
The mind is a pond layered in lilies.
I can't always see through it
staggering through the pitiful corn.
Crown of Bees, Pail of Black Water,
to be of your image—
a limbo of afternoons strung together like cardboard boxes,
a barn on the hillside like a bone.
I wanted to be content in an empty room
far from the din of the articulated world.

Windscape

A great pain strafed the city.

The air was a tapestry weft with cries.

Everywhere, women bandaged
the pietas of soldiers.

They washed their babies with sand.

They slept above enormous knives.

Finally, the sky erupted
with little blue parachutes.

Torn from faces, veils
waltzed across the plaza,

which was like someone
leaving a wedding ring

inside the body of a bride.

Green Running through the Figure

Speaks of something unspeakable—

    wooden, arms long lost,
        one crippled foot peeking
            from a white-flecked dress.

Her face, shorn off—a lunette

$$\frac{6}{6}$$

    half-turned
        to the sleepwalker's painting of fog—

        trees barely audible
           in the ghostspun water.

Because You Refuse to Speak

A hammer sounds
between two mountains.

White butterflies scribble
in tall grass.

A passing cloud.

Out on the pond, a snake
inside a swan glides past.

Phrenology

I

I find an old metal scale in a graveyard,
lay my hand on it for warmth.

I know my hand is heavy—
the other side sails upwards, clanks.

$$\frac{8}{8}$$

Next to me, you read from an old book:
To measure one's morality
map the landscape of the skull.

Carved into the smallest stone—
Beloved Daughter 1860-1861
our little crocus in the snow.

One section of the skull is called *Sublimity.*

I press my palm to the mound.

II

Pools of light drip through junipers.

The ghosts of small animals
dart from stone to stone.

What balances *their* deaths?

A handful of teeth?
An arctic flower?

A madrigal wrung from the bottom of a ravening hole?

I turn my ear to the ground.

III

I remember you standing
over your mother's body, hand

on her forehead, your eyes
growing fern-like.

It still survives
in a fragmentary form of divination.

When I touched your skull, traced
its hills and craters, I saw you

balance a peach on a knife.

IV

The top section of the skull is labeled *Wonder*
and cannot be measured unless the windows are open.

What shape does the soul take when it sails?
An oubliette? A blown-out egg? A disc of light
rising skyward, clanking into wherever there is to get to?

Will it ricochet off the great engine overhead?
Another scale? And who records such things?

I dig a hole by the gravestone with my pen.

V

With knowledge man may judge himself,
thus I've mapped the way—

I lay my head like a hive in your hands.

VI

Late sun and leaves throw
a lace shawl over our shoulders.

Timelines melt in our books.

Soon the moon will bear itself
and we'll long to press our fingers to it.

VII

Already, the hawks have found us.

VIII

Beloved Husband, souls are like birds
flying overhead this very afternoon,

though I haven't seen one of them,
or felt the fluted architecture of their bones,

or held their tiny skulls like walnuts
in between my thumb and forefinger,

I hear them crying just the same.

December

deep in my notebook
*   a moon breaks down*
into smaller moons

Hibernaculum

Stone remembers   '
the sea
that hollows it.

Grottos
in the mind
emptied by grief.

Enter the passage
of flapping hands.

Endarken.

You are blind
and transparent.

You are moonmilk.

You are neck-deep
in cave pearls.

Wintering

All night, hemlocks drop their cones on stone steps.
If the cones were slippers, I'd unlock the latch

for the woman who fled from her home in her nightgown.
From under the purple shade of the pines she'd come

to warm her feet in my hands. If her gown were hemmed
in hailstones, I'd fold it over my shoulder to thaw,

and with my lips, drop a seed under her tongue. We'd fall
asleep listening as the pines mourn the waxwings—

those birds in black masks who huddle on high limbs
passing berries from one mouth to another.

A Bedtime Story

The hunter pierced a young doe, but thought
he struck a birch. He hunted until the winter

sun rested its head on the mountains and returned
home with only a handful of red berries. As the doe's

spirit slipped downriver, she dreamed of the hunter
and his family gathered around a table: one flickering

lantern, the last dried quail, five dandelion roots
laid out like fingerbones, and seven tall glasses of wine.

Poem

The fields are stiff with straws
the dead can scarcely breathe through.

Of snow no one can see the end.

Sweet adversary, inside each limb
countless leaves are curling.

How like a frozen raven I
imagine you.

Layover

A woman tears my ticket with her teeth.

I walk in and out of my body.

I am told my soul has taken flight
like a bird startled by invisible whistles.

I understand it's circling the mountains of Peru,
where spilled water flows back to its vessel,

and the hands of the water-gatherers are blue.

Among Sorrows and Stones

Who remembers the letter
trembling over a flame?

I do. I buried Isolde in her black sail.

Who accompanied the bride with a scar
to a parking lot swept with paper roses?

It was I who gestured to the scissors as she mended.

Who, then, will write a cosmogony bereft of stars?

I will, but first I'll form two tombstones into lovers.

How will I know them?

Wormsongs, wakefulness,
Artillery hauled up a great hill.

Then, with your great lungs, will you fill
the silver petals
of a pinwheel stranded on the moon?

I will not, no, never.

Will you shelter me?

My umbrella is made of rain.

What will you do if I exchange
this ancient tear bottle
for a guitar choked with daisies?

I will gnaw my wrist in the corner until you return.

But what if I devour what I love most?

I will bend over you like a wave bends over a wavelet.

Is this the Hymn of the Pearl to the Moon?

No, far from it.

How will I recognize you?

Red hills and sky
Red hills and bones
Among sorrows, among stones

Will you sit upon my creaking breast?

No, but you will learn to bear anything.

Anything? Even the dollhouse softening by our brook?
The doorways billowing, the wallpaper creeping? breathing?

Yes.

Even the rose-velvet miniature camelback sofa?

Even that.

What about the tiny varnished pie?

Especially the small and the sweet.

And the doll stiff in her bed?
Her pinksweet face—haunted, cauled, bitten?

You will bear it all.

Then blow into the ear she's turned from me.

I will blow into the ear she's turned from you.

The Hymn of the Pearl to the Moon

Cast in your image
            and into darkness

we are luminous nudes

bathing
       in firelight
             by cave pools

mistaking our reflections
             for gods.

THREE

February

tight as Pluto
     as far and as cold

Scarecrow

Inside my chest an apple darkens.

Inside the apple a wind barely sleeps.

Inside the wind hayforks pitch.

I burn with songs of the beginning,
Before birds.

Go back to your life beyond the cornfield,
Back to the farmer's wife and her faraway heart,
To the garden clouded with flowers—

You'll make no friend here.

Estranger

You are a thread
of music

lost—heard,
then lost again,

a song
sewn upon a wave.

I am locked
inside a music box,

battered
by the kisses

of a toy ballerina.

Return

Reverse the plough! Pluck me from this orchard of
bones—from the hummingbird flying backwards

to kiss an orchid. Free the sickle from its rust.
Break the blue cup on a balcony overlooking the sea,

and its enormous envy of the sea, and the sea itself—
its antiphonal call, its ten thousand dead languages

haunting the halls of shells marooned at our feet.
Release the Ferris wheel lying on its side—

half-buried in sand, half-eaten by a slow, salty wind.

Nostrum

Optima dies prima fugit
　　　　　　　　—Virgil

I've tied the hem of your death
to the end of my bed, counted

your hallucinations like sheep.
No bigger than small children,

regrets limp back to sleep
in their bloody socks.

A worm crawls out
from under my lifeline.

When I lean out the window,
Beauty and Time drop from my pockets:

a brooch, a watch, a set
of everything I've lost.

How easily things pass over
into a world we hardly know.

Because the best days are the first to flee,
it's all right to lie down in delusion together—

two strangers
asleep under an apple tree,

dreaming of a tiny cloud
caught in the waist of an hourglass.

Under the Ghost Tree

Leaves, little ghosts,
leaves like handkerchiefs,

white pocket handkerchiefs
wagging in the dark, something

I could cry into—like the palms
of a towering ivory icon…

a cardboard figure
writes into his matchbook

inside a diorama
under a tree made of tissue.

Oracle

I see grave-clothes unfurling inside a flooded coffin,
I see the box loosening in the mud, struggling to surface,
the hand-carved mahogany, the pleated velvet pillow,
the soaking grave-clothes, and of course, the body,
the body fresh inside the box, the hand still soft, falling open
like a lily, the hair ribboning the cheek, the head listing
in the direction of the muddy hole, riding swells down
Harkness Road, the body blushing in the box, the body's
pink earlobes, fingerpads, the body's bracelet of bells
ringing under water, sailing faster now, faster than you think,
the water filling the mouth, black, overflowing, the body itself
stirring, dancing to a bracelet of bells, over tracks stitching
the land, past the goldfish still in its bowl, I see the coffin
rolling, lifting in the current, the cold water rushing in, the body
spinning faster inside the box, the eyelids opening, closing,
the grave-clothes twisting, rising over the poppy and plough,
I see it hovering over this valley.

On Not Finding Your Grave

It's dark,
      the air sick with moths.

Under the canopy
      of the camperdown elm,

God is a barn of blazing horses.

Afterworld

I'm in the far field
slashing
the lupine with my crutch.

My thirst
burgeoning
into a well.

Deer enter, slip
one by one
into the permafrost.

Arrows find their mark
where forests slide
uprooted out of the sky.

Above me, His sprawling
signature of stars—
wheezing like a glacier.

Trying to Pray

O to kiss, once more,
      His watery mouth
            where the first Word
                  was but a solitary cell!

April

from brittle lips—
fireblue butterflies

Before Poetry

I

There was a time when flowers of the field
were flowers of the field and did not fall
from the wandering mouths of strangers.

The apple blossom
was not the nothing in its fatal going.

II

We were not born
sobbing the stories of our deaths.

Once, Muses made love to us.
Once, the Word made flesh.

III

There was a time when nothing stood
for the darkness found only inside bones.

Lucifer meant light-bringer to the blind.

Wolves did not circle anything.

IV

The more I lose, the more symbols I find
and for each I gain, I am less—

Like this
        like this
                like
                this. Like a spore

wintering inside a thimble, like thimbles.

Darkling

They say I shouldn't think of you.

As if you were a piano
        at the bottom of a lake.

The worst I can do
        is turn you into something.

They say I should think of you dead,

though you are a flower
        bursting through armor.

Strangelet

I dream I find you
on my sofa
sleeping

mistake you
for a rifle
laid down gently
until dawn

how silent
my dream of
you sleeping
as a rifle
so sweetly

& perhaps
dreaming

Washing the Feet of the Crucifix

Tethered divers,
we go fathoms down.

I unwind the rope to let Him rise,
hover above me in deep water,

a place I can forgive Him
His barnacled halo,

a place we can bend
in the undercurrents like weeds or hair,

His delicate ankle bone, fastened
in the skeleton of my hand.

Each Light and Shade a Solitude

The artist molds a bony horse
bowing over the lip of a cistern

He pauses

The artist shepherds us into his windscape

He is cruel

The artist's legs are made of glass and filled with tears

He is a lachrymatory

The artist coaxes a ship
from the mausoleum of an iceberg

He awakens

The artist sleeps in an ossuary of parasol bones

He grows tired of beauty

Like trains, like stars

$$\frac{50}{50}$$

The Romantic Sublime

A dress tosses
in the waves
of a painting
as if a woman
still bound
to the corset
of a god-startled sea
flings her hair
back so far
it seems as though
her neck might snap—
which is how much
the easel suffered
buckling
under a lavender sash.

51

While You Were Away

I wrestled a mannequin out of your trunk. She was a mess of
hair and lipstick smears. I think you tried to pierce her nipples
with hatpins. Her eyes—forest green marbles glued deep in
her sockets. They were fixed to the sky, as if she were praying,
or having a fit, or both. No matter how I tried, I couldn't
budge her rigid lids. I tried kissing her full on the mouth. I
slept at her feet as if on the stairs of a silent, white church.
I propped her up and showed an excruciating filmstrip of a
waterfall across my bare chest, but nothing made her see me.
I hope you won't miss her much. She leapt head first into a
river of rented trees.

Daffodil

Daftly ill, and prone to
languid and introspective poses,

I'm haunted by the wedding
of the shepherdess to a caterwaul,

naked vines straining
their infinitesimal mouths,

the somniloquy
of the sleeping asp,

a bloated lamb split
by the strokes of bells,

and three bees sipping
the fragile city
growing on my shoulder.

55

Please forgive me.
I am an ancient man.

I lean upon a great rusted sawblade.

$$\frac{54}{54}$$

The Somniloquy of the Sleeping Asp

I am the little black
      curled inside the lamb.

If the center of the sea forgets me,
      the center of the sea forgets you.

FIVE

August

a bee stung
        and flew forgetful by

In the Room of the Lovelorn

We are not unlike Cezanne
obsessed with a mountain,
painting it over and over
until it is no longer a mountain,
a mountain attached
to foreground or background,
snowcapped or cornflowered,
weatherworn, or born
of quaking earth, no longer
a mountain adorned
with mist and mourning doves,
or careless gleaners
who leave their sickles
in the earth like thorns.

Portrait of the Artist with Rossetti's Sitter

We give too much to those we call Dove or Whetstone or Trumpet Bell.
We blow into their loose sleeves. We imagine them emerging from birches

fingering harp strings, a shell in their hair, a leaf on our sleeve,
a bower meadow dotted with bees. We bury poems on their breasts,

hoping they'll rise from the purgative dark of our waking dreams—
Beau-ti-ful! Beau-ti-ful! Come see the peacocks streaming through
  the nightfields!

But in the end, we slide on our high boots and gloves, and by the light
of a fitful lantern, we dig and dig and dig because we have to
    take it all back.

Pastoral

Fanned out in the night, I hear
the windmill give its life to the wind.

A satellite drifts by, recording
my inner dials.

I think I'm not alone.

All over the world, people lay down
in fields and wait for the sky to open.

Somewhere, our devotion
is being compared on an infinite chart.

Somewhere, we resemble spoons
laid across a table.

Aubade

My bare body
like a handkerchief

dropped
in the blue bower

afflicted
with lacerated flowers

makes a home
of your wasting shadow

the way linnets
weave nests

with strands
of our hair

left reeling
in sweetgrass.

Watercolor Left in a Humid Kitchen

Clearly, she's ruined.

Her face an overripe peach,
her hand a blowzy peony.

In the rising river, a woman
clutches a white bough, this I can tell.

But is it snowing or flowering?
Is she laughing or drowning?

And is that my hand
dragging her to shore by her hair?

Notes from the Boat Docks

As the boats believe
in their sighing boathouse,

and two black dogs struggle
for the same tossed stick,

I have faith the statue of a young woman
(that cast of solitude in the garden)

will one day drop her book of stone,
and forgetting an afternoon of suicide,

step down from the ledge
and dip her fingers in cool bright shoots.

I believe in the hunger of slim bathers,
in the calm face of the daymoon—

65

in the Saint of Lost Causes
as he floats by, face-down

in his clear robe of water,
in the duck feigning a broken wing,

and in the one black dog
as her jaws finally close

around a duckling
in her daydream on the grass.

I believe in passing clouds
as they darken a page of Yeats,

in tiny laughter ringing across the water
like a chandelier of spoons,

in two girls approaching
in rowboats, no longer dolls.

Closer, I can almost brush
the rounder one, blushed

from working the current,
wounded even—like the pear

smoldering
with bees at my feet.

I'd compare the girls to us,
but we are more like the bees—

seized by a dark perfume of things,
thirsty and drowning

together in sweetness
under the red bridge I believe

always within reach
even if you cannot.

Amor Vincit Omnia

When forests wither into scrolls
and dark planets drift by like mourners

when a staircase uncoils from the clouds
and winter buries the garden alive

when the sky finally opens its studded doors
and you lower your locks into erupting rooftops

when the night is awash with angels
and the absence of angels

when sunrise melts your Words into swords
imagine our love is the key to a boathouse

imagine a harbor far off in the distance at dawn
imagine the harbormaster

Restoring the Fourteen Stations of the Cross

I looked down on a mountain, on a cry rising up from the cracked earth. I looked down on the swine and the cattle, and they moaned a little. And I looked down on the tiny beings with their tiny tools, and a few looked back and shuddered. I looked on their blades slung low on their hips, their ropes and whips, their hem-stained gowns, their field of filthy crosses. And it was good. And I looked down then on a shepherd lost. I moved over his path in the dust, and it vanished under my great fist. This too was good. He stumbled. He bled over stones. Everything was as it should be. I painted him pale and thin as parchment. I drained blood from his crown thick and dark like oxblood. In the end, his nimbus crumbled in my fingers. And when he looked up into the firmament—I withdrew from him, from all of them.